A Visit to Town

by John Serrano

This is a house.

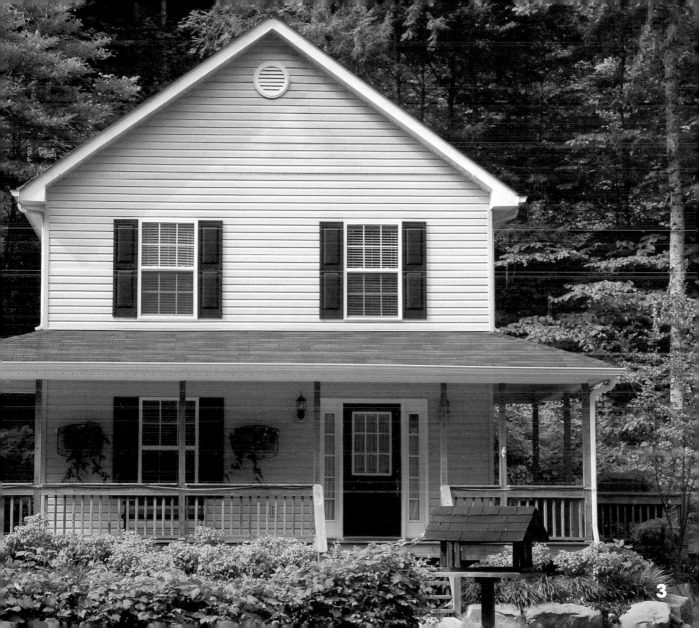

This is a store.

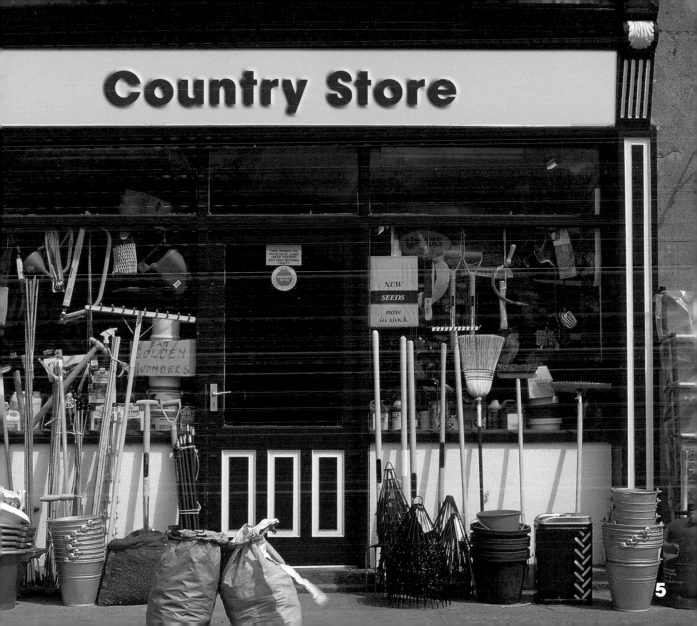

This is a school.

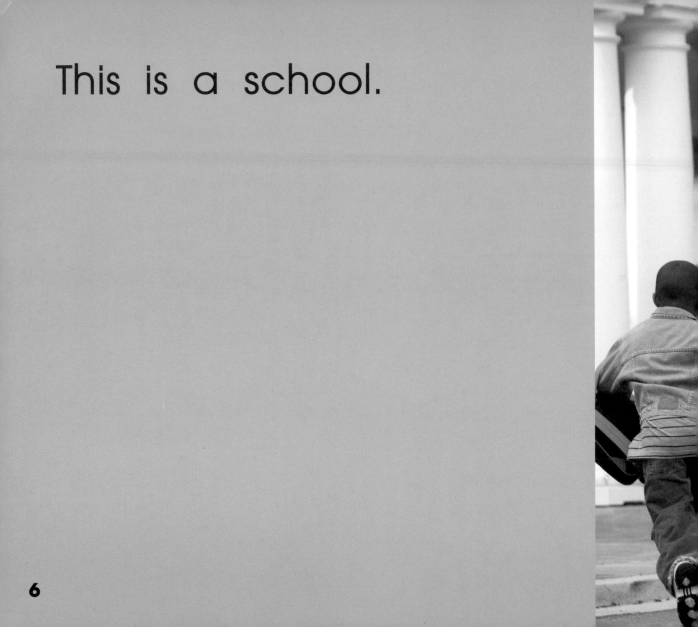

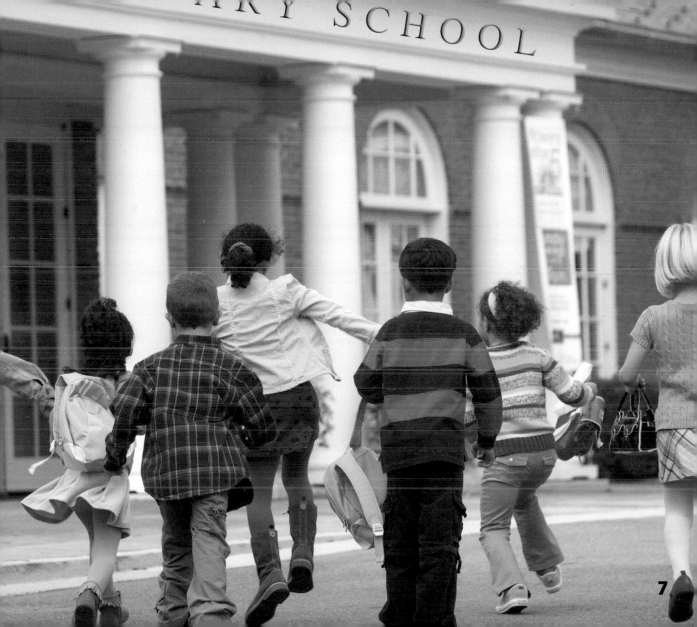

This is a playground.

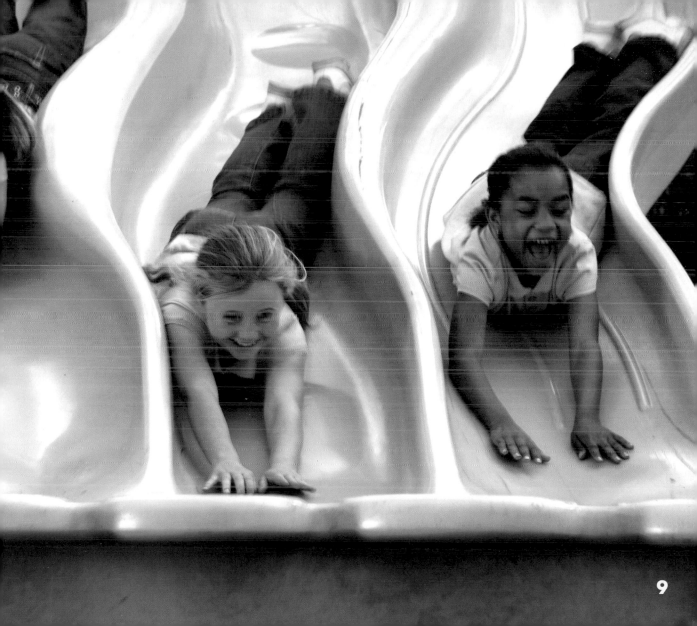

This is a post office.

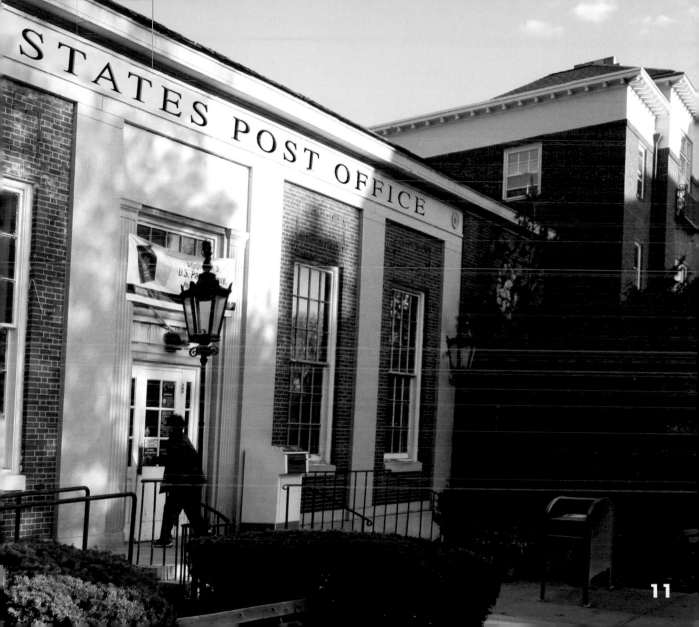

This is a park.

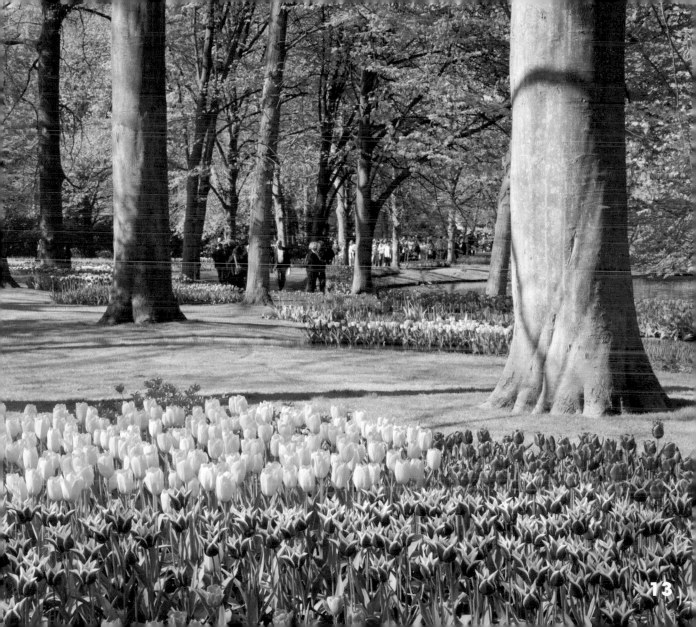

This is a firehouse.

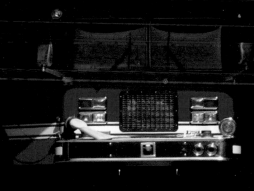

FIRE DEPARTMENT

This is a town!

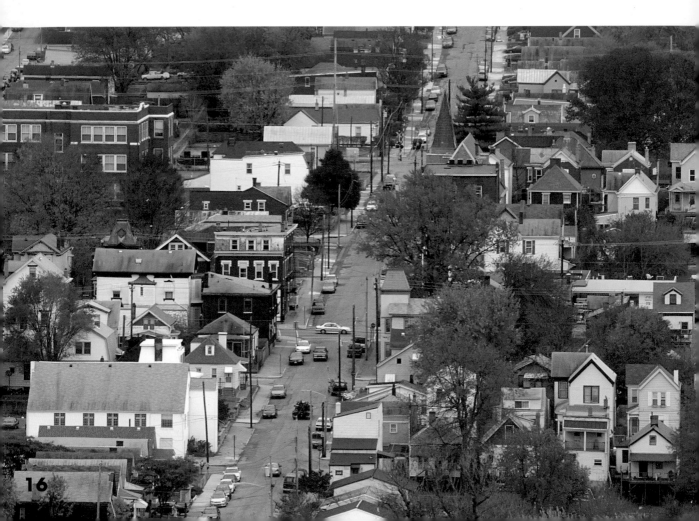